MY PET PUPPY

written by **Marilyn Baillie**

illustrated by **Jane Kurisu**

Kids Can Press

Puppy Pals

Hi! My name is Sunshine and I'm a puppy.

Puppies come in different colors, shapes and sizes. But we all need lots of care and lots of love.

This book is about all puppies, especially your own cute, furry friend.

There are plenty of spaces for you to fill in neat things about you and your puppy. Watch for "Puppy Notebook" sections like this one.

Puppy Notebook

My name is _____ .

I am _____ years old.   I am a ◯ girl   ◯ boy

I have _____ brothers and _____ sisters.

I got this book because

◯ I have always wanted a puppy

◯ I just got a puppy

◯ I will be getting a puppy soon

◯ _____

Your puppy is a member of your family and you can help keep it happy and healthy.

Be on the lookout for awesome "Bow-wow!" sections. You'll find tips and Try This suggestions for special things you can make or do for your puppy. There are even puppy jokes!

BOW-WOW!

Believe it or not, some of my relatives are really wild. As well as the dogs people keep as pets, the dog family includes hunters like wolves, foxes and coyotes.

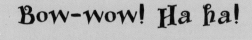

Bow-wow! Ha ha!

How can you keep puppies off the streets?
Answer: Put them in barking lots!

A Great Puppy Pet

I'm a Golden Retriever, a kind of dog that's big, gentle and easy to train. There are many kinds, or breeds, of dogs, and many dogs are a mixture of breeds. Whatever kind of puppy you have, it should be happy and healthy.

A healthy puppy
- has clear, bright eyes
- has fur that is shiny with no bare patches
- has firm, pink gums
- has been vaccinated
- is calm and curious when you hold it

Check if anyone in your family has allergies. If someone is allergic, you can probably still have a puppy, but it might have to be a special breed of dog.

BOW-WOW!

Some dogs are bred for specific jobs. There are herding dogs, hunting dogs, guard dogs, sled dogs and rescue dogs. Golden Retrievers — like me! — make great guide dogs and therapy dogs. But most dogs specialize in being your faithful pet at home.

Puppy Notebook

I'll try my very best to care for my puppy every day.
I'll walk my puppy on a leash _____ times a day.
When I need help looking after my puppy, I will ask

○ my mom

○ my dad

○ my brother

○ my sister

○ _____

My puppy needs its shots to stay healthy. It has

○ had its shots

○ an appointment to get its shots on this day: _____

My puppy is

○ a purebred _____

○ a mix of these breeds: _____

○ a mystery mix

When my puppy is full grown, it will be the size of

○ a bunny   ○ a lion

○ a lamb   ○ _____

Get Ready, Get Set

Going to a new home is a giant step. It's easier for your puppy to settle in if you're prepared for it. So make sure you're ready, with these things on hand.

Play Toys

Puppies love to chew. Be sure to have balls or teething toys that are fairly hard and not small enough to swallow, which could make your puppy sick.

Dinnertime

A clean food dish and a water bowl are all you'll need for feeding your puppy. Find out what kind of puppy food your puppy is used to and have some at home.

Looking Good

Brushing your puppy with a dog brush will help keep its fur healthy and shiny.

A Special Space

Where in your home is your puppy allowed? Your puppy will probably have accidents before it is fully house-trained, so keep it in an area that is easy to mop up.

Sweet Dreams

Your puppy's bed can be a soft blanket in a box or low basket, in a quiet, warm spot that is close to your family activities. A ticking clock or a radio turned on low can be company for your puppy for the first few nights.

Puppy Notebook

Before my puppy's arrival, I collected these things:

- ○ an old blanket
- ○ a box or basket for a bed
- ○ a food dish
- ○ a water bowl
- ○ puppy food
- ○ teething toys
- ○ a brush for grooming
- ○ _____
- ○ _____
- ○ _____

I still have to get these things:

_____

_____

_____

BOW-WOW!

I love to explore new things and new places, and so will your puppy! Please put away anything that might harm your puppy. And tuck away things you don't want your puppy to gnaw on, like your slippers.

Welcome Home, Puppy!

Your puppy's first day at home is exciting for you and a little scary for your puppy. Talk in a soft voice and watch quietly while it explores its new space. Soon your puppy will feel right at home.

Happy Homecoming

Here are some first steps to welcome your puppy:

- Hold your puppy gently and whisper, "You'll love your new home!"

- Show your puppy its bed and food dish, and offer it a small drink of water.

- See what toys your puppy finds fun.

- Take your puppy to its toilet spot. If your puppy uses its toilet spot, reward it with a yummy dog treat. Your puppy will be toilet trained quite quickly if you and your family take it to the same spot several times a day.

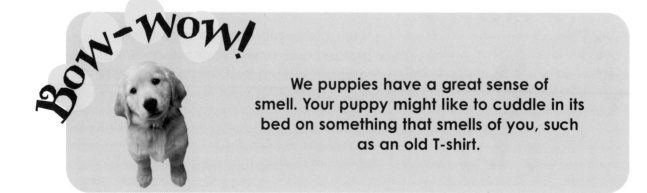

BOW-WOW!

We puppies have a great sense of smell. Your puppy might like to cuddle in its bed on something that smells of you, such as an old T-shirt.

Homecoming No-nos

These are some things not to do with your new puppy:

- Don't leave your puppy outside alone. It could wander away, get sick from other animals or eat something it shouldn't.

- Don't overtire your puppy or make loud noises that might frighten it.

- Be careful not to drop your puppy.

- Don't take your puppy into rooms that are not part of its puppy space. This will only confuse your puppy and it won't know where it's allowed to go.

Bow-wow! Ha ha!

What do you get when you cross a puppy with a chicken?
Answer: A chicken that lays pooched eggs!

Puppy Notebook

On my puppy's first day at home, this is what happened:

When I first put my puppy down, my puppy

- ◯ shivered
- ◯ raced around
- ◯ peed on the floor
- ◯ _____

My puppy's favorite place is _____ .

My puppy is about the size of a

- ◯ baseball
- ◯ soccer ball
- ◯ beachball
- ◯ _____

My Amazing Puppy

Puppy Notebook

Here's what my new puppy looks like. I think it's the greatest puppy in the world!

My puppy's name is _____ .

My puppy's eye color is

○ blue

○ brown

○ _____

My puppy's eye shape is

○ round

○ oval

○ _____

My puppy's ears are

○ long and droopy   ○ tall and pointed   ○ short

○ _____

The color of my puppy is

○ white   ○ black   ○ reddish   ○ brown

○ a mixture of these colors: _____

_____   _____

○ _____

My puppy's coat is

○ long and fluffy

○ sleek and short

○ curly

○ wavy

○ _____

My puppy's nose is

○ flat

○ long and pointed

○ in between

My puppy's tail is

○ long and feathered

○ long with short fur

○ short

○ _____

My puppy weighs _____ .

Bow-wow! Try This

How much does your puppy weigh? Here's how to find out:

1. Step on the scales yourself and write down your weight.

2. Pick up your puppy and stand on the scales holding it. Write down the weight of the two of you together.

3. Subtract your weight from the weight of the two of you (you can get a grown-up to help).

My puppy has these special markings:

Puppy Care

Your puppy depends on you and your family to keep it clean and healthy. We all like to look and feel our very best!

Bath Time

When your puppy is getting a bath, rinse the soap out of its fur really well. Be careful to keep the soapy water away from your puppy's eyes and ears. Then towel dry your puppy and give it a big hug.

Bow-wow! Ha ha!

Why did the puppy jump into the pond?
Answer: It wanted to chase a catfish!

Tooth Care

You can help brush your puppy's teeth. Use a soft toothbrush and use only dog toothpaste, never your toothpaste. Crunching on dry puppy food and gnawing on teething toys helps your puppy keep its teeth and gums healthy.

Grooming

When you are brushing your puppy's fur, tell your puppy how awesome it looks.

Puppy Notebook

My puppy

○ loves having its teeth brushed

○ hates having its teeth brushed

○ _____

When I brush my puppy's fur

○ my puppy wiggles away
   and hides under the bed

○ my puppy tries to nibble
   at the brush

○ my arm gets tired

○ _____

When it's bath time my puppy

○ loves the water

○ jumps out and shakes
   all over me

○ _____

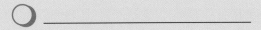

BOW-WOW!

I love going for walks! As your puppy
gets older, you can take it for walks on a leash.
Carry a plastic bag to "stoop and scoop."
Who wants to step in doggy mess on
the street?

Snacks and Supper

Healthy puppies need a balanced diet of the same kind of food each day. There is dog food made just for puppies, full of healthy things for your growing pet. Your puppy will be playful and have glossy fur if you and your family feed it well.

What Can My Puppy Drink?

Pour small amounts of fresh water in your puppy's water bowl each day. This keeps your puppy from gulping down too much water at once. Be sure there is always water, especially if your puppy eats dry food or the weather is hot.

Bow-Wow!

I think people snacks are tasty, but I know they're not good for me. Chocolate and grapes can be especially harmful to your puppy. And no scraps from your supper, please! Your puppy will be too full for its own food — and you'll be teaching your puppy bad habits.

When Should I Feed My Puppy?

Puppies eat several small meals a day, depending on their age. Give your puppy its food in its own bowl, in the same spot, at the same times each day.

Bow-wow! Ha ha!

What do puppies drink at picnics?
Answer: Pupsi-cola!

Puppy Notebook

My puppy's favorite food is _____ .

My puppy hates to eat _____ .

Once I caught my puppy eating _____ .

I feed my puppy _____ times a day.

A Perfect Puppy Day

Your puppy will be happiest if it knows when it is feeding time, toilet time, play time and sleep time.

Here's what makes up a happy puppy day:

1. Early in the morning, after meals and in the evening, take your puppy to its toilet spot. When your puppy goes, give it a dog treat and tell it what an amazing puppy it is.

I hate it when my food dish and water bowl get yucky, and so will your puppy. Wash its dishes with soap and water, then rinse them well.

2. Breakfast, lunch, dinner and snacks should always be the same puppy food and fresh water. It's not boring. It's yummy and really good for your puppy.

3. Now for the best part of the day! Romping around or just hanging out together, your puppy loves to be with you as much as you love to be with it.

4. Ah! Snuggling in a cozy bed! At night, when it's your bedtime, it's time for your puppy to sleep, too.

Puppy Notebook

In the morning my puppy always wakes me up

- ○ by whining or barking
- ○ by sniffing and scratching at my door
- ○ by licking my face
- ○ _____

When I come home from school my puppy knows we are going to _____ .

If my puppy is asleep when I get home, it is usually

- ○ in its crate
- ○ on my bed
- ○ in the kitchen
- ○ _____

When my puppy is hungry, it

_____ .

My puppy's favorite part of the day is _____ .

Sometimes my puppy and I like to do things together, like

- ○ looking at books
- ○ watching TV
- ○ just hanging out
- ○ _____

I give my puppy a hug

- ○ many times a day
- ○ once a day
- ○ _____

One Healthy Puppy!

Your puppy can't tell you if it's feeling sick! Here are some things you can look for when your puppy doesn't seem well.

A sick puppy will
- be very tired and droopy
- have runny or crusty eyes
- have a runny or crusty nose
- have a dull coat
- not want to eat
- foam at the mouth
- vomit or have diarrhea

If your puppy has any of these signs, ask a parent to call the vet right away.

Bow-wow! Ha ha!

What did the puppy say to the flea?
Answer: Bug off!

BOW-WOW!

A regular checkup at the vet's lets my family know that I'm in the best of health and up-to-date with my vaccinations. Shots stop your puppy from catching nasty illnesses. And the vet visit gives your family a chance to ask all their puppy questions.

Puppy Notebook

Here's a healthy puppy checklist.

My puppy

○ wants to play   ○ has sparkly eyes

○ has a shiny coat   ○ gobbles up its food

When my puppy goes to the see the veterinarian, it

○ hides under the chair I am sitting on

○ shows off and runs around

○ _____

My puppy

○ has had fleas

○ scratches but has not had fleas

My puppy

○ has never been sick

○ has felt a little sick

○ had to go to the vet because _____

When my puppy got sick, I _____ .

Barks and Howls

Puppies don't need words to chat. Your puppy talks with its body, especially its face, ears and tail. Its whines, barks and growls let you know what it wants to say. Here are some of the things your puppy might be saying to you.

I'm top dog.

When two puppies meet, they often look alert, stand tall with their tails in the air and stare at each other. They are deciding who is "top dog."

Don't bother me.

Leave your puppy alone if it growls or pulls its lips back to show its teeth. Dogs defend their space this way and your puppy might try to bite you.

You're the boss.

If your puppy rolls on its back, it is giving you respect as its leader or "top dog."

What's up?

When your puppy stands alert with its ears forward, it is receiving sounds to figure out what's going on around it.

You're the best! I love you!

Nose nudges from your puppy and snuggling up to you means "Here I am" and "I love you" or "I want to play with you." Next time your puppy nudges you, pat it and whisper "You're the best!"

Puppy Notebook

My puppy is telling me something when

○ it rubs against my knees

○ it listens and wags its tail

○ _____

My puppy

○ yaps to say this: _____

○ woofs to say this: _____

○ whines to say this: _____

○ _____

My puppy's ears do this when my puppy is angry:

○ point forward   ○ point straight up

○ point back   ○ _____

When my puppy hangs its head, that means _____ .

Puppy Play

Puppies are playful and need exercise every day, just like you. Playing keeps your puppy from being bored and getting into mischief. Try different games and exercises to see which ones you both find fun.

Puppy Ball Game

Throw a tennis ball or hard rubber ball in front of you. Yell "Let's go!" and have a race with your puppy to get to the ball first. If your puppy is very young, run beside it and help it run with you. Now toss the ball again. Off to the races you both go!

Puppy Notebook

Our Weekly Fitness Chart

Monday: we _____ this many times: _____

Tuesday: we _____ this many times: _____

Wednesday: we _____ this many times: _____

Thursday: we _____ this many times: _____

Friday: we _____ this many times: _____

Saturday: we _____ this many times: _____

Sunday: we _____ this many times: _____

Jumping Challenge

Find two or three small, empty cardboard boxes. Set them up so you and your puppy can run and jump over each box. Now do it again. How long can you jump over the boxes before one of you gets tired? Don't forget to count the jumps!

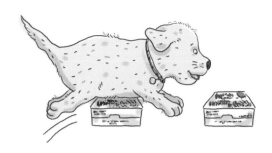

Puppy Notebook

My puppy and I love to work out. Together we can

○ race around the block   ○ run to fetch a ball

○ jump over a box _____ times in a row

○ _____

○ _____

My puppy wants to play

○ always   ○ never   ○ sometimes

The funniest game my puppy plays is _____ .

BOW-WOW!

If you go out with your puppy, make sure it has ID: it has to wear a collar with your name and address, or have an ID chip under its skin. Don't undo the leash because your puppy might get lost or run in front of a car.

Tricks and Training

Teaching your puppy takes lots of patience and lots of love from everyone in your family. Have fun learning together.

Teaching Tips

Here are some tips for your training time together.

- Be kind and firm.
- Use a calm voice.
- Make eye contact for commands.
- Use the same command word every time.
- Add your puppy's name to the command.
- Use love and praise, never punishment.
- Keep the training short.
- Practice the training each day.
- Use a dog biscuit as a reward.

Bow-wow! Try This

My family trained me to "come" by repeating these steps every day. See if you can train your puppy.

1. With my favorite toy in her hand, my person faced me and made eye contact.

2. She patted her legs and said, "Sunshine, come!"

3. When I moved towards her, she gave me a huge hug and a dog treat!

In time your puppy will come to you when you only say the command.

BOW-WOW!

Did you know that I walk on my toes? This gives me extra spring and speed for running.

Puppy Notebook

When I call my puppy's name and say "come" my puppy

○ comes

○ runs the other way

○ _____

A neat trick my puppy can do is _____ .

My puppy likes to do other things, such as _____ .

I would like my puppy to learn to

○ sit

○ stay

○ roll over

○ shake a paw

○ _____

Travels with Puppy

Travels with your puppy can be fun if you plan ahead and if your puppy is old enough to go into the big world.

Make sure your puppy is used to its travel crate or pet carrier. If you are traveling by car, first take your puppy in its carrier on small, easy drives. If you are flying, an adult will make the arrangements for your puppy with the airline.

Don't give your puppy anything to eat or drink just before the trip. It might get carsick or plane sick.

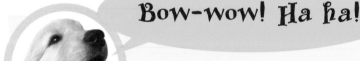

Bow-wow! Ha ha!

Where do puppies sleep when they go camping?
Answer: In a pup tent!

Bow-wow! Try This

Not all hotels or campgrounds are happy to see puppies, no matter how cute we are! Your parents can call ahead to find out if we're welcome.

Puppy Notebook

You'll need this stuff to travel with your puppy. Circle the items as you pack them:

The farthest my puppy has been from our home is

○ next door   ○ across the ocean

○ another city   ○ _____

In the car, my puppy

○ gets very excited   ○ is miserable

○ gets sick   ○ _____

Puppy and Me

My Puppy Scrapbook

Here is a space for my best story about the greatest puppy in the world.

_____

_____

_____

_____

_____

_____

_____

My Puppy Gallery

(Draw or glue in pictures of your puppy. Write down the date and what your puppy was doing.)

Date: _____

_____

_____

_____

_____

Date: _____

_____

_____

_____

_____

Same Time Next Year

It's been one year since I got my puppy, and we both have changed a lot!

Puppy Notebook

My puppy has grown up into a dog, and looks like this:

I look different, too!

I am now _____ years old and am in grade _____ .

Puppy Notebook

My dog knows how to

◯ sit

◯ walk on a leash

◯ _____

◯ _____

◯ _____

What I love best about my dog is _____ .

My dog weighs _____ .

My dog has grown so that its head reaches

◯ my knees

◯ my waist

◯ my shoulders

◯ _____

Bow-wow! Ha ha!

What is taller sitting down than standing up?
Answer: Your dog!

Dedication

For Cali and Christine and all their animal friends

Acknowledgments

A special thank you to Dr. Richard Medhurst for
his expertise and generous assistance.

An appreciative thank you to the following people: Jane Kurisu
for her lively illustrations; my editor, Kat Mototsune, for her creative
and unerring eye; and to everyone at Kids Can Press.

Text © 2005 Marilyn Baillie
Illustrations © 2005 Jane Kurisu

Kids Can Press acknowledges the financial
support of the Government of Ontario, through the Ontario
Media Development Corporation's Ontario Book Initiative, and
the Government of Canada, through the BPIDP, for our
publishing activity.

Published in Canada by
Kids Can Press Ltd.
25 Dockside Drive
Toronto, ON M5A 0B5

Published in the U.S. by
Kids Can Press Ltd.
2250 Military Road
Tonawanda, NY 14150

www.kidscanpress.com

Edited by Kat Mototsune
Designed by Kathleen Collett

Veterinary Consultant: Dr. Richard Medhurst,
Rosedale Animal Hospital, Toronto, Ontario

Cover and interior photos by Getty Images

Manufactured in Buji, Shenzhen, China, in 8/2010 by WKT Company

CM PA 05 0 9 8 7 6 5 4 3

ISBN 978-1-55337-651-4

Kids Can Press is a Corus™ Entertainment company